GRACIE'S SECRET

Written by L   lie Rozzano

Illustrated by Nata   Starikova-Abud

EDGEWOOD PUBLISHING
Part of the Edgewood Health Network

ISBN: 0993740901
ISBN-13: 9780993740909
Edgewood Publishing
Toronto, Ontario
Library and Archives Canada Cataloguing in Publication:
Rozzano, Lorelie, author
Gracie's secret / written by Lorelie Rozzano. — 2nd edition.

ISBN 978-0-9937409-0-9 (pbk.)

I. Title.

PS8635.O99G73 2014   jC813'.6   C2014-904425-9

This book is dedicated to Emma Zannet, a very talented and creative young lady. Emma illustrated the first edition of *Gracie's Secret*. She inspires her friends and family alike with her artistic style, wise words, and big heart. Without Emma, *Gracie's Secret* would not have been possible.

Grace yawned and rubbed her eyes. Her little brother Cameron was nestled against her. He was five years old and could be a real pest. But most of the time, you'd never know he was there. Cameron had the saddest eyes she'd ever seen. He had bad dreams. Sometimes she did too.

Grace had a secret. One she'd been keeping for years. It was more of a feeling, really. And it felt . . . bad. "Cameron," she said, poking him. "Get up," she warned, worried that Dad would be mad if they were late for school.

While Cameron got dressed, Grace made the bed and hurried downstairs.

Mom was in the kitchen staring out the window. Her face looked funny. Grace studied it, noticing how tired she looked. "Hi Mom," she said.

Mom frowned as she turned away from the window to look at her. "Hurry and eat your breakfast. You don't want to be late for school."

Grace poured a bowl of cereal for her and Cameron, but neither one of them could eat very much.

On the way to school
she ran into one of her
best friends, Abby.

Abby wore a red jacket and a great big smile.
"Hi Grace!" she said as she skipped along beside her.
Grace tried to smile back, but it wobbled on her lip.

Not noticing, Abby asked, "Can I come over to your house after
school today?"

"No." Grace shook her head. "Mom's not feeling well." She felt bad for
lying, and her stomach hurt. She wished she could tell the truth, but she
didn't want Abby to know about her parents' fighting, or that she wasn't
allowed to have friends over.

After school Grace walked home as fast as she could. As she neared her house she spied Cameron in the front yard, smashing his truck into the tree.

She bent down, taking the truck from him. "You're going to ruin it," she warned.

Cameron stared at the tree, his shoulders drooping. He rarely spoke. Grace wondered if he had the bad feeling in him, too.

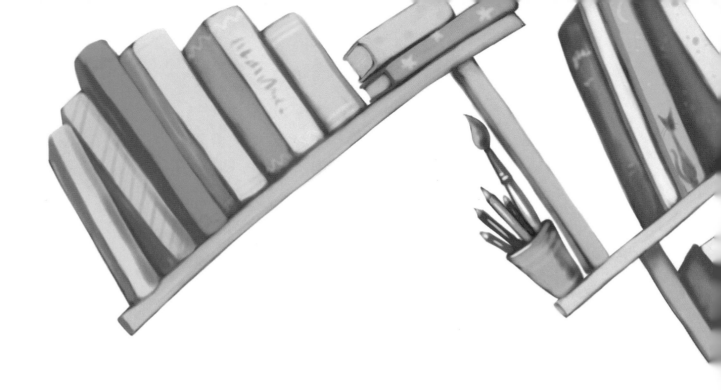

On tiptoes she entered the house. Her head felt funny. Sometimes she forgot to breathe.

Grace ran up the stairs and into her room.

She liked to pretend. In her pretend world, her mom would be happy and smile a lot. Her dad would like children and spend time with her. Cameron would be a chatterbox, and she would be the most popular girl in school. Her parents would never argue, and her stomach *never* hurt. Maybe if she wished hard enough, she could make her pretend world real.

The next day at school, Abby asked Grace to come to her house for dinner. Grace raced home to ask. To her surprise, her mother agreed.

As she knocked on Abby's door, her stomach flip-flopped. She wondered if she'd be able to eat anything. For a moment she thought about going home. Before she could leave, Abby's mom opened the door and smiled at her. "Hello Grace," she said, giving her a hug. Grace stiffened at the unfamiliar embrace. Abby's mom let her go. "Come on in. It's so nice to see you!"

Confused, Grace studied Abby's mom from underneath her lashes. She seemed very happy to see her, and Grace couldn't understand why. She hadn't done anything special.

At dinner, Abby's family all sat around the kitchen table. Grace watched Abby's dad cautiously, waiting for the fighting to start, but it didn't. Instead, he joked with his family.

She began to feel strange. The room grew warm. Her hands became sweaty, and she started to shake.

Her glass of milk slipped from her fingers and spilled all over the table. Grace gasped, staring in horror at the mess.

Her shoulders tensed as she waited for the explosion, but it never came.

Abby's mom gave her a new glass of milk. She stopped as she caught sight of Grace's face. "Don't be upset," she said, patting her on the shoulder. "It was just an accident."

Grace wished she could dive under the table and disappear.

Abby's dad smiled at her and asked, "Why so quiet, Grace? Cat got your tongue?"

Alarm ripped through her. *What should she say*? Grace hoped dinner would be over soon.

That night, Grace fell asleep thinking about Abby's weird family.

Loud voices woke her up.

Her stomach dropped and she shivered. Her bedroom door creaked open, and she spied Cameron, trailing his blanket.

"Gracie," he whined.

The voices downstairs grew louder. Her parents were at it *again*.

Cameron climbed into bed whimpering next to her. The bed sheets grew damp and warm.

"Oh Cameron!" Grace cried, grabbing the extra blanket from the bottom of the bed.

Covering the wet spot as best she could, she consoled her little brother.

"Everything will be fine. You'll see. I can take care of us," she promised, no longer mad he had just wet the bed. Besides, she knew how he felt. She might not wet the bed, but sometimes she hid under it.

Grace wished she could take Cameron and run far away. She held him close and hummed, hoping to cover the noise of their parents' yelling so he could fall asleep.

Her stomach was hurting again.

The raised voices below them were joined by a crash. She plugged her ears.

Her bedroom was so dark she thought it might swallow her up.

Grace closed her eyes, trying to stay calm as she imagined what was going on downstairs. Her eyes blinked back open, not able to stay closed. She remained upright in bed for most of the night.

The next day at school was awful. Time seemed to drag on forever as she fought to stay awake. Her head was too heavy for her neck, so she rested it on her desk.

The ringing school bell woke her up. Her cheeks grew hot as she glanced around the classroom wondering if anyone had noticed.

Her eyes locked on Ms. Taylor.

Oh, no!

Grace looked away from Ms. Taylor, but not before she saw the frown cross her face. She stood up, intending to flee the classroom, but Ms. Taylor's words stopped her.

"Grace, could you please stay behind? I'd like to have a word with you."

Her heart sank. Her stomach hurt. Her thoughts raced. What had she done wrong? Her dad would be so mad if he found out about this!

Ms. Taylor sat down next to her. She smiled and said, "Thank you for staying behind."

Grace blinked and squeaked, "Am I in trouble?"

Ms. Taylor looked at her thoughtfully. "No Grace, you're not in trouble. But I did want to ask you a question. Is everything all right?"

"Everything's fine," Grace lied, her face growing red.

"I'm concerned about you. I've noticed how quiet you've become," Ms. Taylor said, speaking softly. "You've lost your smile. Is something bothering you?"

She didn't know what to say! No one had ever asked her that question before. Grace, who had become very good at making things up, found herself unable to say anything.

A lump grew in her throat. Her vision blurred, and a warm, fat drop landed on her hand. She stared at it in horror. She was crying! Grace scrubbed her eyes, trying to stop.

She'd always gotten in trouble for crying, but Ms. Taylor didn't get mad. Instead she asked, "Would you like to talk about it?"

"I never have." Grace sniffled.

Ms. Taylor smiled. "Talking is good for you. You make yourself sick when you keep everything bottled up inside. Our bodies weren't designed to hide our emotions. That's why we have words."

"But my words don't always come out right. They get mixed up and . . . I'm not supposed to tell," she finished with a rush.

"What happens when you keep your words and feelings inside?"

Grace was stumped. She'd never really thought about it before. Her brows furrowed in concentration. Then a familiar pain in her stomach interrupted her. An idea began to form, and she whispered, "My stomach hurts."

Ms. Taylor nodded. "That's right, Grace. My stomach hurts too when I hide my words and feelings."

"It does?" Grace was amazed. She'd thought she was the only one.

"Everyone has problems. Sometimes, when we live in families where we've learned to keep our words and feelings hidden, it becomes a habit. That's why it's very important to find *safe* people to tell those words and feelings to."

"What's a safe person?" Grace asked.

"A safe person is an adult you can trust. Someone you can confide in and who will help you. It can be your school counsellor, your doctor, or a friend's parents, or a grandparent."

Grace thought really hard. "I don't think there's anyone safe I can talk to."

"Sure there is, Grace. You're talking to me right now."

Grace took a big breath. "I'm afraid you might laugh at me. Or see me cry."

"I'm not laughing," Ms. Taylor said gently and then asked, "Why are you afraid of me seeing you cry?"

Eyes wide, Grace exclaimed, "Because *crying* is for babies!"

"Grace, crying isn't *just* for babies. Do you know what our tears are really for?"

"I know they're very annoying!"

Ms. Taylor shook her head and smiled. "Most people think tears are just for cleaning our eyes, but they have a far more important job. Sometimes worries and hurt can get stuck inside our bodies, making us feel heavy and weighed down."

Grace thought about her parents arguing.

"Our hearts can become hardened over time." Ms. Taylor paused and looked at her. "Just like a scraped knee that grows a scab. It changes who we are, or who we might have been –"

"How does it change us?" Grace interrupted.

Ms. Taylor thought for a moment. "We might stop smiling, or grow quiet. Some of us get angry or become bitter. Others simply stop caring. But tears are smart. They wash these painful feelings away . . . *if* we let them."

A tight band in her chest let go. She wasn't exactly sure what Ms. Taylor was talking about, but her stomach didn't hurt anymore.

A few moments passed before she could speak, and when she did, she surprised herself.

"Ms. Taylor?" Her chin quivered as she looked at her teacher. "I'm sad."

Grace clapped a hand to her mouth, but it was too late. Her secret was out, and she couldn't take it back.

Once she started talking, she couldn't stop. Words poured from her. Tears spilled down her cheeks, only this time she didn't try and stop them.

Her tears went to work, scrubbing furiously. She worried that she might cry forever, but she didn't. Her tears simply finished their job, and stopped.

Grace realized she needed to get home. Torn between wanting to stay and needing to go, she hesitated.

Ms. Taylor smiled and opened her arms.

Grace took one step, and then two.

She wound her arms around Ms. Taylor's waist. She didn't even feel stiff when her teacher hugged her back. Warmth blossomed in her chest. It was nice to feel cared for.

As she said goodbye, she felt different . . . lighter . . .

Free.

On her way home she thought about all the things Ms. Taylor had said. The problems in her family weren't her fault, and if she didn't keep her words and feelings buried inside, she would be all right.

Grace laughed, giddy with relief.

She'd told her secret.

Only to have learned the biggest secret of all!

After you read *Gracie's Secret:*

1. What do you and Gracie have in common?

_____

_____

2. Gracie's stomach hurts when she keeps her painful feelings inside. What happens to your body when you do the same thing?

_____

_____

3. How do you act when you feel nervous, scared or worried?

_____

_____

4. What do you do when you're angry?

_____

_____

5. What other ways can you find to express your feelings?

_____

_____

6. Ms. Taylor teaches Gracie about safe people. Who are three safe people that you can talk to about your feelings?

_____

_____

_____

About the Author:

Lorelie Rozzano is a recovering addict. She is also a mother, sister, grandmother, foster parent, wife, and daughter. Lorelie works a program of recovery herself, and understands first-hand the benefits of a healthy family. She began working at Edgewood Treatment Center in 1998 and has had the privilege of working with both patients and their families. In the past few years, Lorelie has written three fiction books: *Gracie's Secret*, *Jagged Little Edges*, and *Jagged Little Lies*. Her hope is that the honesty of her books will help those dealing with unhealthy behaviours and addiction. Lorelie is currently working on book three in the Jagged series. Learn more about her books at www.jaggedlittleedges.com.